SAND AND SKY
Poems from Utah

SAND AND SKY
Poems from Utah

RUMI PUBLICATIONS
an imprint of
RUMI POETRY CLUB
2017

Sand and Sky: Poems from Utah

Copyright for this volume © 2017 Rumi Poetry Club
All rights reserved.

ISBN-13: 978-0-9850568-2-7
ISBN-10: 0-9850568-2-7
Library of Congress Control Number: 2017902537

First Published in 2017
RUMI PUBLICATIONS
Rumi Poetry Club
P.O. Box 521376
Salt Lake City, UT 84152-1376
Email: info@rumipoetryclub.com
Website: www.rumipoetryclub.com
Facebook: www.facebook.com/rumipoetryclub

Front cover painting by Setsuko Yoshida inspired by southern Utah's landscape
Back cover photo of a scene in central Utah by Rasoul Shams

Printed in the United States of America

DEDICATION

This volume is humbly dedicated to poets who have contributed to the environment, culture, and literature of Utah.

***

How do you place a value on inspiration? How you quantify the wildness of birds, when for the most part, they lead secret and anonymous lives?

Terry Tempest Williams in *Refuge*

CONTENTS

Preface 13
1. Coyote Communion 15
2. The Last Revival Meeting of Autumn 17
3. Summer Song 19
4. Speak, Spirit 20
5. Summer Corn 21
6. Button, Button 22
7. Singing to the Soul 24
8. Burial Grounds 25
9. Mandella 26
10. Obituary Addendum #7: Dylan at Practice 27
11. Sanctified Flight 29
12. View from Here 30
13. Gypsy Beads and Falling Fronds 31
14. Abandoned 33
16. Where is Home 34
17. Touche' 35
18. A Natural Man 36
19. Cemetery Visit, Koosharem, Utah 37
20. Saturday Specials 38
21. The Moon's Salon 39
22. Silhouettes and Shadows 40
23. Moving Out 42
24. Early Morning Love Poem 43

25. Rot, Moss, Cedar...44
26. Sand Waves...45
27. Canyon Calling 46
28. Mother of My Bones 48
29. At Dusk 49
30. Woman with Basket 51
31. Turquoise Memories 52
32. Abandoned Amphitheater 53
33. Stolen 54
34. Scattered Sleep 55
35. Ascension 56
36. Ayurnamat / It Cannot Be Helped 57
37. New Revelation 58
38. The Desert Wind 60
39. Counting Coup 61
40. A Gathering of Bones and Feathers 63
41. Springtime – Great Salt Lake 64
42. Quik Stop 66
43. What Are You Going to Do? 68
44. Climbing up the Wasatch Mountains 70
45. Untitled 71
46. Even My Bones Are Singing 73
47. Deseret, Utah 75
48. White Gloves 77

49. Spring in Southern Utah 79
50. At Piute Reservoir 80
51. Downside 82
52. Grandma's Peace 83
53. Life's Prayer 84
54. Desert Pupil 85
55. Connecting 86
56. My Father's Photographs 87
57. My Mother's Eyes 88
58. What My Son's Robot Drawings Teach Me 90
59. Aphorisms for a Lonely Planet 91
60. Oh! Our Love! 94
61. Blue Sentinels 95
62. A Singular Vermilion Sky 96
63. Colors on the Hill 97
64. The Silver Lining of Fish 98
65. Objet Trouve 100
66. Memories of Long Ago 102
67. Coast to Coast 103
68. Brave Pioneer Women 104
69. Near Moab 105
70. Dripping Hours Flow 106
71. Mary's Reverie 107
72. I Will Be "Til I Die 109

73. We, Desert Dwellers 110
74. Bees After Scorpion 111
75. Performing Myself in the City Where I Lived Before 112
76. A Meeting 114
77. Kristallnacht 115
78. The Girl Lost in Time 116
79. Sipapu 118
80. A Mountain in the North 119
81. Irony 121
82. Birdsong 123
83. For a Dead Fawn on the Highway 125
84. Das Heilige 126
85. Fly 128
86. Sand and Sky 130
State Symbols 131
Short Biographies of Contributors 133

CONTRIBUTORS

Margo Andrews	*15, 17*
Roger Evans Baker	*19, 20, 21*
Vera Ogden Bakker	*22, 24*
Marilyn L. Ball	*25, 26*
Shanan Ballam	*27*
Cindy Bechtold	*29, 30, 31*
Neil Bowen	*33, 34*
Doug Brewer	*35*
Markay Brown	*36, 37*
Marleen Bussma	*38*
D. Gary Christian	*39, 40*
Tyler Clark	*42*
Anastasia M. Clarke	*43*
Brock Dethier	*44, 45*
Stacy W. Dixon	*46, 48*
Fae Ellsworth	*49*
Lin Vernon Floyd	*51, 52*
Bonnie Glee	*53, 54, 55*
Lynne H. Goodhart	*56*
Sylvia Ruth Gray	*57*
Dawnell Hatton Griffin	*58, 60, 61*
Maurine Haltiner	*63, 64, 66*
Lindsay Jane Hanks	*68*
Alina Hansen	*70*
Rebecca Holt	*71, 73*
Lorraine Jeffery	*75, 77, 79*
Grace Diane Jessen	*80, 82*
George King	*83, 84*
Kate Kirkham	*85, 86*
Marjorie Kyriopoulos	*87, 88*
Lance Larsen	*90, 91*

Satyam S. Moorty	*94*
Florin Nielsen	*95, 96, 97*
Joel Passey	*98, 100*
Gail M. Peterson	*102, 103, 104*
Patricia Peterson	*105, 106*
Susan Randall	*107, 109*
Susan Roche	*110, 111, 112*
Natasha Sajé	*114*
Eva Sanchez	*115, 116*
Meghan Nuttall Sayres	*118*
Rasoul Shams	*119*
Carolyn W. Taylor	*121*
Melanie Rae Thon	*123*
Howard Nelson Tuttle	*125, 126*
Linda Waters	*128, 130*

Acknowledgments

The poems in this volume were selected from a large number of poems submitted by various contributors. The following served as the selection committee for the poems:
Margo Andrews
Florin Nielsen
Rasoul Shams

We are grateful to all those who contributed their poems to *Sand and Sky: Poems from Utah*

PREFACE

Place connects people. Books are bridges.

In 2009, on the centennial celebration of Wallace Stegner's birth, the Salt Lake City Public Library hosted a screening of *Wallace Stegner: A Biographical Film Portrait*, produced by KUED Television of the University of Utah. The film was later also broadcast on PBS. While watching the film at the library with several hundreds of people, these two lines took a vivid life in my mind: Place connects people; books are bridges. There we were – people from various walks of life connected by the place and Stegner's books about the spirit of time and people in Utah. Stegner (1909-1993), often regarded as the "dean of Western writers," grew up in Salt Lake City and graduated from East High School and the University of Utah. If you walk at Library Square downtown Salt Lake City, you can see this quote from Stegner inscribed on a brick wall: "Culture is a pyramid to which each of us brings a stone."

Poetry is like food: good poetry nourishes our souls and inspires our minds. This anthology of poetry from Utah, published on the tenth anniversary of Rumi Poetry Club in Salt Lake City, aims to present the spirit of place, time and people as well as expressions of life and love in Utah. The title *Sand and Sky* should not come as a surprise: After all, Utah is a land of sunny days, blue sky, and red sandstone. Here again we have an inspirational line from Stegner: "Nowhere else in America are such great blocks of nearly level strata lifted so high above broad, deep valleys. Nowhere else would we see forests along such lofty rims" (*American Places*, p. 115).

Maps are among the things I love. I know maps do not show the real sandstone, the sky or the sun. But maps are about culture as much as they are about landscape. People who have contributed to the culture of a region have also contributed to its physical map. The map of Utah, for instance, is not merely the product of geographers and explorers but also of Mormon settlers and pioneers and native Indians – the Utes, Shoshones, Goshutes, Piutes, and Navajo people. A map is a product of land and life. In this sense, one may also include the fauna, flora, and rocks as contributors to the construction of a map. A poem is also a product of life; it is a map of heartscape. This integration of nature and culture is apparent in the pages of this volume. In this spirit, I hope, readers will enjoy this collection of poems from Utah.

Walt Whitman called his poems *Leaves of Grass* and added that "I believe a leaf of grass in no less than the journey-work of the stars." That is the power of poetry.

                                            Rasoul Shams
                                            Director of Rumi Poetry Club
                                            Salt Lake City
                                            January 2017

1. COYOTE COMMUNION

*"The grief you cry out from draws you toward union.
Your pure sadness that wants help is the secret cup."*
                                                    Rumi

What is the sound my soul is making?
It's the howl of the hole in my heart.

I'm empty of the love I once knew and
full of hate for the creature that raided the nest and
shattered the fragile eggs to suck out the life.

Alone in the cold desert and unable to stand,
I lie down and press my body against the sand for heat.

I am determined to stay at this point and not run away.
Aching, disconsolate pain.
Only the throbbing tells me I'm still alive.

Blood drips from my wound
into the cup that will not pass me by.
Sacrifice. Accept my sacrifice.

And then I hear it.
The holy howl of a lone coyote mourning its other.
I throw back my head and join the beast in
the deepest sound my being has ever known.

Howling until we are both spent,
we are utterly alone and utterly united
in this strange communion.

Peace be with you…
And also with you.

Margo Andrews

2. THE LAST REVIVAL MEETING OF AUTUMN

There's a dervish in the hills today.
Picks up speed as He turns 'round and 'round.
Tunnels of leaves twirl to earth.
Trees tap their roots just keeping time
once more before they are still with frost.
Feel the pulse..
the heartbeat of spirit in motion.
The sky a kaleidoscope
of the face of the one
who made us.
A lens of infinite whirling.

Clap your hands!
Ring the bells!
Shout the news!
Praise the Lord!
Throw open the doors,
church will be outside today!

Joy unbridled,
Peace unending,
Undone,
Unleashed,
Unrestrained
WHIRLING!

Brown and white,
white and brown.
 Storm clouds fill
and start to burst.
God comes to earth.

The mystic cries:
"I can dance and whirl and fly!"
"SO CAN I!" the echo calls.
So can I. so can i.

Margo Andrews

3. SUMMER SONG

(Walking on a farm road, called Rabbit Lane, in Erda, Utah)

Ground-line sprinklers in the green alfalfa hay
make such pretty music,
like the field song of crickets and katydids
on a hot, summer evening.
Cows' tails swishing in the tall, dry grass,
and the breeze fluttering stiff poplar leaves,
add apropos percussion
to the sublimity and song.

Roger Evans Baker

4. SPEAK, SPIRIT

(A moment of reverie in Snow Canyon State Park)

Great Spirit,
Father of earth and sky—
manifest Thyself unto me.

Spirit Son,
Child of earth and sky—
see my writing in the rock,
in the swirling veins of cemented sandstone,
in the lichens' greens and grays.
Hear my voice in the warbles and trills of song birds,
in the lonely quail call.
Smell my wisdom in the breeze-born sage
after desert's summer shower.
Taste my nature in the pure water
pooled in pocks etched in stone over a million years
by grinding wind and splintering ice.
Touch my mind as you touch with whisper touch
the stunning, delicate cactus bloom,
as you cause the fine red sand to sift through wondering fingers.
Feel my heart as you cry
and reach for the sky
at sunset.

Roger Evans Baker

5. SUMMER CORN

(An experience in my Erda, Utah garden)

Lay with me between the rows of summer corn.
Don't speak, yet.
Listen
    to the raspy hum of bees gathering pollen from pregnant, golden tassels,
    to the hoarse soft rubbing of coarse green leaves in the imperceptible breeze,
    to the plinking rain of locust droppings upon the soft soil.
Listen
    to the neighbor's angus wieners bemoaning their separation,
    to the pretty chukars heckling from the chicken coop,
    to the blood pulsing in your ears, coursing through your brain.
Don't speak, now.
Reach to touch my hand.
Listen to the world
from within the rows of summer corn.

Roger Evans Baker

6. BUTTON, BUTTON

A red, white and black Calumet
baking powder can, its belly full of buttons
sat on the shelf during my growing years.

Buttons of all colors shapes and sizes.
Buttons with two holes, four holes or shanks
on the back for sewing to the garment.

Buttons held great imaginings and memories.
Perhaps this one came from Dracula's cape
or *this one from my favorite first grade dress.*

We sometimes substituted buttons
for lost game pieces, and they conveniently
covered numbers on Bingo cards.

Before an expired dress or shirt was buried
in the rag bag, all salvageable
buttons were donated to the can.

After laundry day, Mother searched the can
for buttons that matched, *almost,*
those lost in the weekly operation.

The heavy old flat iron came in second only
to the wringer washing machine
in the conspiracy to destroy buttons.

Today I wear a T shirt,
jeans with an elastic waist,
and eat muffins from the bakery.

Vera Ogden Bakker

7. SINGING TO THE SOUL

When David plays his harp, he calms the fear
of Saul. *Thy rod, thy staff they comfort me.*
When Christ is born, the lowly shepherds hear
an angel chorus sing for joy, of *peace,*
good will toward men. When tired babies cry
and can't be soothed, the mothers rock them, save
the quiet night by crooning lullaby,
now *sleep my child and peace attend thee.* Slaves
in shackles pull the oars, sing, *yo-o heave*
ho. Families picking cotton keep their hope
alive with song, *do Lord remember me.*
Sweet serenades tempt maidens to elope.

For me, I find relief in hymns, *abide*
with me, fast falls the darkest *eventide.*

Vera Ogden Bakker

8. BURIAL GROUNDS

For a little while the night and day
lived together and I in it.
The stars of my dreams could shine
blessing the river with reflections
of their early night beauty.

With my flesh and bone I visit ashes of my father.
There I walk with my dead, memories
carved upon the sacred slate of my mind.
Time moved the willows, the wind
sang a soft song to my people.

I heard the red stone hills speak to me --
with voices of wisdom, a recitation,
a lament, filled with deep love for our history
and the land. Their words and whispers
send me forward, suddenly brave again.

Marilyn L. Ball

9. MANDELLA

He stands remote, this stoic Plains Indian.
A warrior wrapped in his pride, his 'old ones'
chant and sing while he is blessed.
He has used the vision of his manly test
to guide him, now the sacred songs.

Nearby in a sandy circle is painted hidden
meaning for his quest. He searches for perfect
willows, bends them to a circle while his hands
imprint a message that only he knows—the fur
and rawhide accepts, will last many moons

He hefts its taut fit, feels it divide the winds, circles
it into the sky, chants, makes it part of him and earth.
To this, his mandella, he sings his song, then ties in eagle
feathers, the blessed bow points and his mother's hair.

Marilyn L. Ball

10. OBITUARY ADDENDUM #7: DYLAN AT PRACTICE

Dylan, Dylan,
when I was thirteen,
on the Junior High volleyball team,
I hauled you in your baby carrier
to the gym. I held you aloft
and all the girls stopped, stunned
by your dimpled smile —
they rushed to touch you, kiss you,
pinch your plump cheeks —

We tossed you in the air, tickled by your squeal,
by the arms we swung you in stumbling circles —
we held you high
in the shine of the gym,
like the prize we'd never win —
Nikes squeaking on blonde gloss,
fresh sweat glistening flushed faces —
everything beginning —
you aloft, smiling,
the youngest,
held above everything,
a little silver spittle on your pink, pink lips —

later, in the dark, I cradled you,
felt your greedy suck collapse
the plastic bottle in my hand.

In your ninja turtle pajamas
you staggered
into the dazzling hallway light —
luminous, you,
before you slipped away.
Forever I will see
you standing there, drenched with light.
My youngest brother,
my golden trophy

        Shanan Ballam

11. SANCTIFIED FLIGHT

Her arm brushes the bundle of savory tied to a string
as she winds the mantle clock for seven more days.
The andirons, forged by her father, rest on the hearth.
Dusting the cupboard, she stops a moment,

running her finger 'round the lantern rim—
oil reservoir filled to the brim, wick trimmed.
She places starched doilies over the arms of the chair
full knowing everyone must leave luxuries.

Wiping mama's condiment set she sighs.
In the bedroom, she picks up her hand mirror,
squeezing a blue atomizer into the air.
His boar-bristled brush dries in the earthen mug.

Picking up the broom she sweeps back and forth
with the cracks, paying close attention to the grooves.
Scooting a tin whistle from under a stool, shrill notes fall
from her lips to her pocket, not much extra weight to pack.

Driven again, masses of Saints prod oxen, horses,
or their own tired feet, fleeing from hostility.
She shuts the door and joins the rest,
the broom left leaning in its place.

Cindy Bechtold

12. VIEW FROM HERE

The moon agrees it's weird out there.
Kids dressed like vampires, ghosts, and bats.
If they could only watch from here
those freaks and fakes would disappear.

That one kid's mask falls off his ears.
Shrek drips green clear down his chin.
Those creeps aren't real, no need to fear.
Hauntings don't occur near here.

Parades of ghouls, and clattering boos,
fake witches, teeth, and jelly-blood goo,
blue dragons, frogs and eerie tattoos.
Fairy wands, magic, and tricks are for fools.

Now look at me, a majestic tree.
True from the start, no make believe stuff.
Get back to the facts and let all this be.
You people get real here, no pretending for me.

Okay, I must admit at times I cave in
to the smells of cider, spices, and sweets,
to the rush of the evening, the sound of the wind.
But don't you dare try to squeal on me.

It seems, I secretly loooove—Halloween.

Cindy Bechtold

13. GYPSY BEADS AND FALLING FRONDS

I park my car by an awakening willow tree and walk,
the headstone visible from the road I travel each day
now only a few yards away.

No season is ignored. The planter sways
on its stand through summer's solstice,
apple autumns, winter wind, spring breath.

No holiday dropped, custom décor rotates inside:
miniature flags and sparklers burst
above pansies on Independence Day.

No ghosts acknowledged on Halloween
only princess crowns and gypsy beads
grace acorns and spider mums.

Nestled in boughs splattered with snow,
Santa's cheeks puff berry red,
elves and reindeer nestle in open air.

Floral picks tipped with hearts shoot
from depths on Valentine's Day—greens trailing,
Cupid's plastic arrow pointing heavenward.

In spring, tulips' vested heads bow to Easter Lilies,
bunnies bobble on painted picks hidden amongst
molded eggs too small to hold jelly beans and things.

Rusty stand guards the headstone,
fronds covering her death date.

Cindy Bechtold

14. ABANDONED

awkward metal sits in the corner of the field
the mowers cutting blade reaching towards heaven
once shiny-now frozen with rust
never to work again
monument to the past
the harrow sits a few feet away
large tines once resilient
fragile with age
soon to return to the earth
one rust flake at a time
slowly over years it happens
old ways abandoned
some call it progress
others decay
alfalfa once groomed
now grows wild

Neil Bowen

16. WHERE IS HOME

There are places where
Earth and land beckon me back
I'm at peace
My core quiet
Conduit dirt to sky
Even there, after a pause
Alone I'm restless
There are places I go to get whole
In the pines or desert
Communing with sunsets
Cleanses my soul
Space opens
Thoughts clear
Still I become restless
Because of your love
Home is no longer a place

Neil Bowen

17. TOUCHE'

"Dear Clara," the young cowboy wrote,
      "My memory's starting to go.
I proposed to you last night and didn't note
      If you'd said yes or no."

"Dear Will, how nice of you to write.
      My memory's going, too--
I knew I'd said no to someone last night,
      But I'd forgotten who!"

Doug Brewer

18. A NATURAL MAN

Aspiring master of the untamed land,
he lives to scout, explore where few would dare
to venture: silent places near the end

of earth. His city friends would condescend.
But solace is his goal, a classroom where
he's ardent student of the untamed. Land

and open sky his simple home, yet grand,
a castle without mortgage or repair.
He worships silent places near the end

of wildness, rock cathedrals God will lend
his soul when trials loom and hope is rare.
He knows the Master of the untamed land

is greater than himself, a perfect Friend
worth knowing, so he visits places where
in silence, he can get to know the end

from the beginning. Pristine hinterland,
this earth of balanced water, sun, and air--
gifts from the Master of the untamed land.
He prays that silent places never end.

Markay Brown

19. CEMETERY VISIT, KOOSHAREM, UTAH

A pink tin pig hand-lettered in black
records Bridgett's entrance and exit,
strange in this place heavy
with cement and marble.

Purple Heart Hero, Max and his Blanche
share a monument to love, not war.
Their chosen words from Goethe:
*No one could ever love
in the same way after us.*

Day-old Rachel died the summer of 1890:
Darling, we miss thee,
words for my own unnamed baby
lost before I held her in my arms.

Wind in the cedars hums a requiem
for the living who visit the graves,
who wonder back to life the babes,
the mothers, the soldiers, the lovers
belonging to all of us.

Hope is chiseled granite-hard,
and a gnarled lilac shields a psalm
engraved on rain-washed limestone:
*Be still and know
that I am God.*

Markay Brown

20. SATURDAY SPECIALS

Carl Wilke owns a grocery store.
He has more money than most
and can afford to hire help.
His customers grudgingly co-exist with the Depression
whose dust has draped their dreams in dismal gray.

Fridays herald sale day Saturdays.
Mute criers typed on sheets of white paper
promise local farmers featured items will cost less.
Each sale bill is wrapped like a cocoon
around its ballast and readied to be dropped
from Mr. Wilke's two-seater plane.

Young Emma spends her summer running barefoot
on her parents' farm.
Late on Friday afternoons
she listens for an engine's drone,
the anticipated precursor to an edible delight
as Mr. Wilke flies over the farm near the big lake
and drops his Baby Ruth bomb.

Marleen Bussma

21. THE MOON'S SALON

In the stillness of a midnight hush,
the silver moon with its silver brush
paints the earth with argent light
like day appropriating night.
With the clouds, the moon retrieves
its essence mirrored on the leaves
when the soul of earth below
is hidden from its magic glow.

The taintless stars as heaven's fonts
present like evening's debutantes
along the hollow of the sky
across the realm where comets fly,
and in the way of charm nocturnal
claim an elegance supernal,
marked primally by all the sages
and lover's vows throughout the ages.

In the solitude of night,
the breeze takes respite form its flight,
sprightly fairies come to play,
to dance along the Milky Way.
And when they weary of their sport,
they vanish all, with out report,
then flit away in to the air
and leave the moonlight shining there.

D. Gary Christian

22. SILHOUETTES AND SHADOWS

Sometimes when day has gone to bed,
I walk along the thoroughfare
attended by an evening sigh,
trolling with a velvet snare.

Far across the heavens watching
with her satin-stringed guitar
cuddled by a breeze, love sends
her message in a shooting star.

I seek her in the evening, waiting,
the author of desire's treasure,
calling in a siren song
with mystic harmony and measure.

But hauntingly her image comes
and just as hauntingly it goes
into the past of yesterday
as wistfully as wind that blows

along the waste and hurries on
into a realm I cannot find
amid the footprints of its sound
across the meadows of my mind.

I find her where the day protrudes
but fear that she will go, too soon,
into the shadows of the night
wooed by the softness of the moon.

D. Gary Christian

23. MOVING OUT

It's been a long time since Eden,
following the tattoo
of a compass
in the flesh of your arm.

You may have the word
"dreamer" written in your ribs,
but my rib was ripped out,
the wound is a scabbed abscess.

I won't see this landscape
of your naked chest again.
Because everything I own is in my car.
My books, my guitars, my clothes,

my material life. How convenient
would it be to die now,
embalmed with my belongings,
my lust, wanderlust, and longings?

Tyler Clark

24. EARLY MORNING LOVE POEM

early dawn
fades into grey

i carried your name
into the pale
winter morning

the sound
of the waking birds
touches skin
to skin

A. M. Clarke

25. ROT, MOSS, CEDAR

(After W.C. Williams)

Old age is
the swamp by the 8th fairway—
chase your errant ball
and you're up to your knees
in muck, sucking your shoes,
dredging the smell of decay,
the sound of slop.

On the mound of an old stump
you rest, dry
on soft green
surrounded by the croaks of frogs.
Dragonflies hover around your head,
the ball, the silly game
forgotten.

Brock Dethier

26. SAND WAVES

Sand precipitates faster
than river can flush it,
silt wall growing upstream,
cresting, whitewater splashing
as though bounced from subsurface boulders.

Sand waves threaten nothing.
3-foot peaks and troughs melt into burbles,
standing rollers dominate
then dissipate, rapids erased
then riled again into riffles and ribs.

Like hoar crystals
layering into moist wind
or plaque in my arteries,
building with every pulse of blood,
the silty river clogs itself.

I wish I knew where a counter-argument
builds beneath the surface,
when a wave is about to break upcurrent.
My kayak T-bones each wave,
cushioned by moving mud.

Brock Dethier

27. CANYON CALLING

I stand on the last
crag of rocks,
darkness eating my fingers
as the mountain takes sun.

I remove my shoes,
pay homage
to ancient feet,
those who looked across
this giant bowl before me.

None can speak an unholy word here,
on the brink of this place,
where surely
voices of the gone
still ring back and forth
without end.

They listen,
these voices,
for the right question.

I should yell out
with my best magic voice,
but as the sky draws her blanket
over me,
I wonder whose voice
will answer back.

Stacy W. Dixon

28. MOTHER OF MY BONES

You have something
to do with this.
I feel it in my bones,
feel you in my bones.

You send pieces
of yourself to me.
In dreams,
or maybe
through an open window.

I feel it in my bones,
feel you in my bones.
Things from there,
you could not do here
with a broken body.

Stacy W. Dixon

29. AT DUSK

Words are odd
filled as they are with merangue
and the ineffable:
stigmata
pragmatism
clank
sleight-of-hand
the muddle and slosh of it all.

They wait on shelves for us to discover
Dance in the dust of movie-theater flicker
Seep through suds
at the kitchen sink,
steal into our hearts
as we sleep.

Transform to starlings,
swim across sky in flock
ballet cape to behold,
murmuration louder now
laid against gold sunset
like frozen pipes moaning a swelling
of motion, of childbirth
prodding their aperture closed
from the hungry hawk.

Far away now, the sound is a needle
insinuating itself into a linen handkerchief,
tatting around the edges.
Below a man driving a truck with a sign on top: WIDE LOAD
sees the shadow in the sky,
looks up.

Fae Ellsworth

30. WOMAN WITH BASKET*

Standing still, wrapped in
the warmth of morning sun,
the Indian woman prepares for
another day of necessary labor,
clutches a hand woven basket
full of corn to grind for meal.

Stoic—weather beaten,
survival is her daily path.
Part of the continuing journey,
alertness keeps danger away
living simply outdoors
providing for loved ones.

Threatened by natural forces
she fears seasons and storms
depending on the land
for sustenance and shelter
hardship is a constant companion,
she knows no other life.

Lin Floyd

*Name of sculpture by Bert Garcia in DSU Sears Gallery in St. George, Utah

31. TURQUOISE MEMORIES

turquoise treasured by ancient ones
        reminders of generations lost to time
red rock desert sands cover their memories
        carefully painted pictographs fade as
drumbeats disappear in the distance
        leaving echoes of traditions long forgotten

dancers in intricate rituals whirl together
        dressed in hand crafted clothing
families dwell in primitive shelters
        surrounded by pungent sagebrush

desert smells linger in the dry air
        as corn, beans and wild rabbit
mingle in campfire stews
        washed down by precious water
turquoise colors reflect sunset's farewell
        to another day of tribal survival

Lin Floyd

32. ABANDONED AMPHITHEATER

This time without you
I climb cracked steps
filled with crushed leaves,
take a seat on deserted
row of weathered wood.

Under moon's spotlight
I hear Chopin echo
in violin-branches
of elm, maple, and pines.
Musical breeze arouses
a percussion of performances
by moths, mosquitoes, fireflies.

I silhouette from seat
descend to center stage
and dance myself
through a summer's dream
back into your arms.

Bonnie Glee

33. STOLEN

You stole my soul with unkind words and sneering
then heaved it like a snatched pair of sneakers
over a utility line . . .
Useless
Forgotten
Irretrievable.

You took my forever-smile, tossed it to the wind
to sway by knotted white laces above
pointing fingers . . .
Alone
Empty
Broken.

You didn't know renewal of dawn would ease
strain on tight ties until tension loosened
tangled hold to . . .
Release
Forget
Forgive.

Bonnie Glee

34. SCATTERED SLEEP

Where are you stretching, yawning,
waking, into nature's window
for another day?

My eyes search for you, people of the street,
as I sashay through daybreak's traffic
safe and warm in black Buick.
I drive block after block with the sun
as it peeks over vi-a-ducts, park benches, church stairwells.

A part of me
envies your freedom from time clocks,
corporate politics, schedules;
imagines you lingering in local library through
long morning hours with words
of many masters until your
stomach purges with human hunger.
I picture you gathering your meager belongings
off marble floor beside comfortable couch,
putting on your prize winter coat
ready to face the many tasks of survival.

I force myself from such heavy thoughts
that see you rummage through back-store dumpsters
or curl up beside warm pet at busy mall exits
with sign, 'will work for food'.

Oh, I see you scattered everywhere.
But tell me,
where do you sleep?

Bonnie Glee

35. ASCENSION

Why should we grieve that we've been sleeping?
We're groggy but let the guilt go
Feel the motions of tenderness around you,
The buoyancy....
             (Rumi: *Like This*, translated by Coleman Barks)

The sun's our yeast today
Everything we see is rising

Over there, the Wasatch range
Drifts upward, weightless as
Opaline clouds, breath of earth
Ascending through
A resonant sky

Houses here are smiling
Washed in crystalline light
They tug at trees
Like boats barely anchored
Bobbing up on waves of sun

I try to hold my hands down at my sides
But they keep lifting, pointing:
Look! The sun's erased our shadows
We are rising in the light

                    Lynne Goodhart

36. AYURNAMAT / IT CANNOT BE HELPED

Mother: In another time you might have taught us
the old ways, might have embodied tribal wisdom.
But for now, all times are at their end and I am sad.
This was not the plan.

First when you asked, we said, "No, be here with us,
under the hides in the warmth called home." When
you asked again, it was, "Be at peace, be full, be
staid; we have much caribou, much fat."

That would have been the end of it, but for your
last and third request. By custom, we have
acquiesced. Yes, you wanted change. Yes, you
wished for rest. Yes, to a speedy, spectacular

death. Here is a cover, the color of snow. This is
the bed; it will feel like ice. And something to chew:
tasteless, like sinew. So, Mother, you have your
riches, and we are bereft as you leave to move

astride worlds, to drift between planets, to go in at
the door of our unknown/your gnosis. And when
He comes as He will, disguised in the skin of polar
bear, hidden in the waves as high as buildings, or

striking from the ocean of the heavens with the shriek
of falcons, I know you will be deeply
cooperative/receptive, and take Him to yourself and
love Him – the Trickster, the Magician.

Sylvia Ruth Gray

37. NEW REVELATION

"And he that sat was to look upon
like a jasper and a sardine stone"
                                    Revelations 4:3

It must have felt like pain,
that first moving gash of sand,
The East Wind digging fingers deep
inside the desert's sculpted veins
cutting arches, pinnacles,
constructed cities of rock.

The heart of the earth is sapphire,
but at night, God put out the light.
Beyond the canyon rim,
the jasper stones glitter,
untouchable in the night sky,
moving across the galaxy.

In the silence of great expanse
ached the mystery of the Deep.
Never ending edges shuddered.
Imagination stretched outward,
inward, larger than thought,
more truthful than belief.

The earth is a Sardine Stone,
a single jewel in the crown.
Molten lava and blackened smoke,
whispered promises. Blessings
multiplied, incomprehensible
like numbering grains of sand.

Genesis, from Haran and Canaan,
covenanters singing of this new desert
home, *Come, come to Zion*.

Dawnell Hatton Griffin

38. THE DESERT WIND

Leisured Adagio
chisels pieces of sand.
Crimson mudstone
beckons,

Come barefoot.
Feel it burn, round
and white as a kiln forged
moon, searing pieces of sky,

hot breath drying out
eternity, the earth shifting
while we stand here
praying for rain.

Taste the fragrance
of the sage, pestle ground.
Listen to the wind,
scorched and dried

rattle across the valley floor,
scrape against our under-bellies,
whisper softly in our ears
until we turn to dust.

Dawnell Hatton Griffin

39. COUNTING COUP

In small, dusty, western towns,
Cowboys and Indians, cattle ranchers
and sheep herders flickered in the movie
house, spoke drawl and pidgin.

In real life, wagons were roll-about camps.
Herders, chap-tied and bow-legged, baked sour
dough, Dutch-Oven dumplings and peach cobbler.
Dogs barked solo. Sheep mumbled chorus.

Cows were herded on horseback, down the Crooked Lane,
then home again. Pahvants, Mexicans and Whites sent their
children to school. Nelda's mother cooked refried beans, tortillas
and traded for my mother's baked bread.

My playmates translated Spanish to English. My uncle's wife,
a native born El Salvadoran, taught me to say *por favor*
and *gracious*. Blanche and Rachel whispered Pahvant.
Cattle ranchers cussed and the Bishop spoke Sabbath.

I know the glassy jangle of spurs when a man walks,
the smell of sweat and the creak of a leather saddle.
My brothers hunted jack rabbit and coyotes with a .22 rifle.
I never saw a six-shoot except John Wayne's.

One of the Pikyavit boys got a job with Columbia pictures.
He got paid a whopping three dollars a day, but only when
he let out a whoop and fell off his horse. Neither Native American,
nor Mexican, still, I learned to count coup on the Silver Screen.

Dawnell Hatton Griffin

40. A GATHERING OF BONES AND FEATHERS

Flesh creeps off with age, like anger
after rage, reveals knobs, bridges, ridges—bones
I can hug and rub anew. No longer
rounded off, my body pokes at all its edges,
stretches as it never has before
to touch the world.

Bare feet pinch sand, just short
of oyster magic. Hands knead snug dirt, feel
the wonder of worms in darkness.
In the shimmer of sun-stunned blue my shadow
leans on petals of one red rose. Mimicking
spots of moss, I find solace
in the sanctuary
of shade.

But, oh, to make a cricket-leap, feet
no longer stumped by gravity. I'd find the wind
and not let go, gather feathers
in flight—cardinal-red, finch-fine, hawk-wide—
hitch them between fingers, toes,
teeth clamped tight. I'd angle some from ears,
tangle others in locks of hair—a multitude
of plumes to wing me high. Buoyed up
by all my hollow bones, I'd fly

in waves of air
where love & peace collide
above the grasp of fragile flesh.

Maurine Haltiner

41. SPRINGTIME – GREAT SALT LAKE

Marsh grass & willows sponged
salt flats, left
sand dry, barren. Wasatch peaks welcome
sun's double
dose of light & reflection
to coax fresh water
from iced ridges. Drops silver
down, underground,
carry scent
of ginger from China, wiffs
of Russian sage, beads
of Sugarbush nectar bolted
from fisted waves
off the Cape of Good Hope— all sprinkled
with cosmic dust eager
to meet a star.

I wait for this rush of life,
this May spill
of streams & rivers that swallows
beaches, rejuvenates
avocets, bald eagles & stilts. Snowy egrets
appear in a flash of wings, poise
in shallows, silent
as pearls they left behind
in oyster beds
off the coast of Louisiana.

I cup
my hands,
receive the seasoned water.

Maurine Haltiner

42. QUIK STOP

We disturb the leisure
of nowhere with our naming. Towns
know themselves only for our sake.
A mountain lake needs
no name to cuddle
cutthroat under shady edges. Cutthroat
know the names of nothing
as they surface at sun's rest, leaping
and plunging into the bull's-eye
of ripples.

Bill at the Quik Stop
Points west. No sign post, but we can't miss
Big Elk Lake with its rack
of inlets.
He rings up twelve
night crawlers, for luck
drops a baker's dozen
in the bag.

We wait with lines out, hope
we've found the spot. No lazy laps
of water break the silence, only
tip clicks of lodgepoles slender
in the breeze. We seek certainty, a sign
to make somewhere here.

As if cactus should care where it eats
sun, ice where it begins
to crack,
or you and I
where we first tasted night, heady
under billions of stars.

Maurine Haltiner

43. WHAT ARE YOU GOING TO DO?

There's no time for this I tell you
I can't wait for time to end
It's coming up over the bridge now
casting doubt over the hills now
Slipping past dappled streams
and creeping beyond evergreens
losing touch with everything
speaking without real meaning

And what are you going to do?

Waiting for the sirens' call
succumbing oh you weak-of-heart
misinterpret ancient dreaming
scramble for that distant breathing
Oh for false encumbered sleeping
Catching empty with
the star light

And what are you going to do?

Void in nets of twisted gape-ings
Reeling from the pangs of hating
Somewhere while the moon is laughing
Once wet desert soil's cracking
Stabbing with untold feeling

SAND and SKY: Poems from Utah

Whispering, "reject your lasting"
how to be a heart that's beating
when your thoughts are always bleeding
out

so what are you going to do now?

Lindsay Jane Hanks

44. CLIMBING UP THE WASATCH MOUNTAINS

I didn't want to touch the sun
but the heat licked me clean.
Burnt epidermis peeled away
leaving a trail. Birds gathered
the fluttering remains
to weave into their craggy nests.
Nestled against the incline
of jagged boulders between the canyons decline.
The dirt ground up
into dust lifts to fill
my nose, my mouth, my hair.
The valley dips,
a wide bowl
that holds
rusted souls.

Alina Hansen

45. UNTITLED

Layers of intimacy
deeply embedded
in forest floor
smells of fallen bark and holly

Gray and white silhouettes
winter encaustic
rusted churches
hustle and bustle
seasons turn

White pine resin
spinning ruse
beating down
chunks of memory
flooding in

Taken
wile without pause
no refuge
frozen moon

Stolen view
from within raindrops
she weeps

The soul's golden nectar
stripped from her insides
like summer never existed

Wasteland
sitting in for the horizon
landscapes of frozen lullabies
haunting the shadow

Edges of marsh and narrow
broken mandalas
circling inside themselves

She begins with a whisper
to utter herself out of this vignette
seascapes of inner miles

All of these threads
being woven
into history
her story
longing melted

Shattered open
she is golden honey
being spun
into infinite prisms of light

Rebecca Holt

46. EVEN MY BONES ARE SINGING —
THIS IS HOW POLLEN SOUNDS

This inner world
casts a shadow on me
once reeling in the shade of things
now there are no echoes
the light is dancing in its own labyrinth
painting siren sounds with each breath

What is this faint rumbling
she is being fueled now
by the fullness fire
at her core

Sunshine hasn't plucked my tongue this way before
hints of geranium petals and grapefruit resin
preaching white peonies
freedom prayers

Contentment sings like wild grace
blue water current
humming down my spine

Even the clouds are speaking in tongues
the lightest touch
feels like blankets of leaf droplets at dawn

All of this stillness
a summer home for the senses
billowing harmony
weaving seasons
through the songlines
in my skin

Rendered anew
the sounds of simple wonder
gently resting now
breathing earth
in the canyons of my bones

Rebecca Holt

47. DESERET, UTAH

Wagons dispatched from Salt Lake
               to windswept flats of greasewoods,
    and rabbit brush.

There was a river, of sorts,
               and a dam to be built.
               Three times it broke.
    Crops were still born.

Fields were sloped to drainage ditches.
               Run-off for the white death of alkali,
               to let green shoots break
               rock-hard soil.

But they, of the wagons,
               stayed.
               Water shared,
               stubble burned in the spring.

Fields greened—
               wheat, hay, barley.
               Houses built while
               tumbleweed blew down streets
                       where children played.

SAND and SKY: Poems from Utah

The church was full
        of rumpled suits and cowboy boots.
        But head gates and water turns
        led followers to furrows.

They imported schools,
        farm equipment,
                and dairies.

        Exported posterity,
                missionaries,
                and heritage

                      Lorraine Jeffery

48. WHITE GLOVES

For Maurice Abravanel
Jewish conductor of the Utah Symphony for over thirty years

Framed in gold, he hangs above their young heads,
above their stiff posture in the lacy dresses and stiff black pants,
above their smooth arms clutching satiny violins.
He stands straight-backed but comfortable in
his black tuxedo and white bow tie.

He approves of the quick breaths
and flying nimble fingers.
His has danced on keyboards in
Berlin, Paris and New York.

But then, in the high desert valleys of Utah,
he chose to shape an orchestra,
and a community, with a baton.

Now he looks out under lined brows
at the young of the valley
earnestly playing Beethoven and Mahler.

He stands above them and remembers Milaud and Stravinsky,
the National Medal of Arts and the Tony Award.
He remembers when he couldn't pay the concert master,
or the cello player,
or himself.

Years in Greece and Switzerland have faded.
He has given his years to this people
he never become part of.

He stands, overcoat draped over his arm,
holding white gloves
gazing over sleek heads,
listening.

Lorraine Jeffery

49. SPRING IN SOUTHERN UTAH

Smoke snakes into the crisp blue sky.
Wisps from Moody's farm, Nielsen's farm,
and ours.

I smell the hot green of the ditch banks
burning autumn bindweed.

Kosha and milkweed writhe, curl and scorch
under bent and blackened cedar posts.

I pull my jacket close and see splats of snow
on the alkali-covered ditch bottoms.

Two fields away, the green tractor whines steadily,
white gulls land on mounds of new brown,
finding insects ripped from the hard desert soil.

Ready for the rush of water,
from mountains I cannot see.

Bounty held back by dams and head gates,
carefully portioning out life.

Lorraine Jeffery

50. AT PIUTE RESERVOIR

Pale green sheets of water rush from the arched
spillway of Piute Reservoir, pour into the river,
churn past flat rocks along the bank. From here,
the Sevier continues its journey, flows through
valleys where my ancestors settled and I was born.

Nearly a hundred years ago, my grandpa
and his father came with other men to build
this dam. They drove their teams of Percherons
pulling wooden scrapers, dragged dirt
from the valley floor to create a mountain
ninety feet high, twelve hundred feet long
at the crest, from rocky ledge to solid hill,
enough to hold the river back,
enough to endure the buffeting of time.

For five years, they toiled here from harvest
through winter's chill to planting time, took
summers off to tend their fields. They hoped
to provide irrigation for planting more acres
in years to come. Ignoring blisters, bruised knees,
they wedged each rock into place by hand
to form the rip rap on the upstream face
of the dam, a giant jigsaw puzzle protecting
precious earth from gnawing water and wind.

I am drawn here by prospects of pleasant hours
with family, trout for supper. Foamy torrents
roar into the riverbed below the dam. Fishermen
cast out their lines, willows bend with a breeze.
Gulls swoop from the cliff above, their cries
echo a song of gratitude in my genes.

Grace Diane Jessen

51. DOWNSIDE

When you are gone,
mornings lose their luster,
the shower leaves me chilled,
nothing in the closet fits,
my oatmeal tastes like mud.

When you are not here,
days drag, work multiplies,
mail is all bills, my schedule
unravels in confusion, my mind
crashes like a frozen computer.

When you are away,
evenings are empty as eggshells,
all the TV shows are reruns,
darkness descends and little sounds—
scurrying, creaking, fluttering—
magnify my fears.

When you are absent,
night is an endless tunnel,
the hands on the clock keep
getting stuck, pounds accumulate,
the mattress develops new lumps,
sirens wail, dogs bark,
some foolish, useless stranger
is sleeping in my skin.

Grace Diane Jessen

52. GRANDMA'S PEACE

As I rush up the lane to Grandma's kitchen
I can smell her new-made bread.

Brushing back her hair, Grandma places
brown loaves in a straight row.
They dare me to taste them.

Grandma chuckles, "It's not ready."

"Ah Grandma!" I press myself against her big white apron.

"Well, maybe just one piece.
Don't you grumble if it crumbles!"

Grandma deftly slices the hot bread,
spreads on home-churned butter,
layers on golden honey
and lays a piece on my plate.

Gobbling, I devour too soon
and look up, eager.

Grandma answers with a wink.
"This time, you stop to taste it."

Years later noises blare around me.
Voices seek to confound me.
Grandma's name's now carved in tombstone grey,
And now I savor grandma's peace.

George G. King

53. LIFE'S PRAYER

May I grow wiser growing old:
Life has so many truths to teach
May I seize upon them and reach
Ever farther, more truth to hold.
May I grow wiser growing old.

May I grow softer growing old:
Life matters less, yet so much more.
Much good is past. Much lies in store.
May I accept life, and endure.
May I grow softer, growing old.

May I grow younger, growing old:
Gladdened and strengthened by the youth
May I smile their smiles & sing their truths,
Following the paths they lead me to.
May I grow younger, growing old.

May I grow bolder, growing old:
With less to risk, sooner to die,
Let me stand firm and learn
To fly as high as any soul can fly.
May I grow bolder, growing old.

May I grow fuller, growing old:
The fires of life within me burn
May I nourish them and learn
To hold tight to all the good there is to hold.
May I grow fuller, growing old.

George G. King

54. DESERT PUPIL

I find your hidden moon lit path
collect nature's bread-crumb wood pieces
huddle against the still sun-warmed rock
searching for a place for fire before your coldest hour.
I am your pupil.

Dressed to wait
rehearsing what I know
to keep sane – safe from your searing heat:
taught by creatures tolerated in your terrain
and the remains of those who would not learn.
Mindful of your illusionary power,
I am your pupil still.

I seek buried history
that only you could preserve,
to protect what we can learn
knowing that I risk your patience
with my presence.
Still, I am your pupil.

Kate Kirkham

55. CONNECTING

She walks
cautiously placing on her aunt's marker timid, spring
Daffodils soon shifted by the shallow breeze to other graves.
She remembers nit-picking summer family stories
from their desert garment of wind-shifted sand and shrub.

Tough marigolds and last-day sunflowers
taunt a memory of fall foliage shimmering
in the gold rays of a favorite canyon sunset.
Barefoot now she wishes to stand
in the salty sand of the Great Salt Lake--
where nature's holographic memory would display
the Pavilion and her aunt dancing.

Moving among the head stones
her being sustains the cord of lives
from ancestor to newly born.
A child in worn out shoes rushes forward to
trace his father's marker.
His future strengthened by the presence of his past.
She walks
holding a flower from her grandfather's grave.

Kate Kirkham

56. MY FATHER'S PHOTOGRAPHS

I am fascinated
by his photographs,
stuffed away in dusty drawers,
waiting for me to pick them up,
one by one.

It's my father,
the photographer,
who draws me there,
as I slip into my parents' bedroom,
kneel down in prayer pose,
and open the bottom dresser drawer,
where I find myself,
cradled in my mother's arms.

She is smiling back at him
like she'll be there forever--
as though the photograph is enough
to keep them together.

Marj Kyriopoulos

57. MY MOTHER'S EYES

I'll always remember my mother's eyes—
the way she squints
even when she smiles,
like she's angry at the world
for all the pain that pushed its way into her heart.

Did giving birth
to an Elvis impersonator and five strong women
take its toll on her eyes, "windows to her soul?"

Did being married to my father,
a man with a million plans
and a knack for executing them,
one at a time,
put that worry in her eyes?

Did the death of her sister,
shot in the heart by her husband,
in a deer hunting *mishap*,
work its way into her psyche?

Did she inherit the pain in her eyes
from *her* mother and father
who brought it with them
from El Greco?"

I see my mother's eyes in my sisters' eyes,
my brother's eyes, and mine.

Sometimes I see her eyes
in the eyes of my children,
my sibling's children,
and her great grandchildren.

My mother's eyes
are an heirloom we carry with us,
a genealogical gem – as hard to penetrate
and precious as the sapphire stone
in her mother's wedding ring,
the one I now wear
every day.

Marj Kyriopoulos

58. WHAT MY SON'S ROBOT DRAWINGS TEACH ME

that a metallic face gleams brighter than anything human,
that skin is the loneliest of kingdoms,
that one giant claw is better than a pair of legs,
that hovering robots rarely perform angelic acts,
that robots lack boy parts and girl parts,
that a lack thereof does not equal androgyny,
that going solar is the latest idolatry,
that hawk robots outnumber dove robots 7 to 2,
that sometimes a violin disarms better than a grenade,
that the "lullaby energy" of a gold watch induces sleep,
that some androids hang out in knitting shops,
that seven mouths recycle garbage better than one,
that the soul can't be drawn but we must draw it anyway,
    sometimes as circuit board, sometimes as tentacles of light.
that burning the dead equals mercy,
that crematorium robots purr while doing their duty,
that their smoke signals resemble a French novel of the air,
that Boomaclonka carries *bossa nova* into the street,
that Cupid-tron makes us fall in love,
that someone's robot has to shrink heads, why not his?
that doing so is as easy as baking pie,
that rain water, scrubbed of toxins, is the nectar of gods,
that most of us prefer to gargle darkness,
that somehow somewhere someone will save us,
that a violent story well told trembles like prayer.
                      after Chard De Niord

Lance Larsen

59. APHORISMS FOR A LONELY PLANET

1
That far-flung hitchhiker, desire.

2
Following a storm, rainbows and bedewed roses—and worms on the sidewalk, most of them smashed.

3
One of those epiphanic moments when I'm so certain the rolling field is my body and the sky is my breathing that I refuse to answer to any epithet but Infinity. Then someone calls my name and I turn.

4
The past is a boneyard of nows.

5
We measure death not as the crow flies but as the buzzard circles.

6
Most of us worship the same way we decorate, by procrastination. Our Halloween ghosties hanging in a tree are just in time for Christmas so we call them angels.

7
He who waits on one Muse writes but little.

8
Two kinds of people fill the world: those who believe maybe just maybe unicorns are real and those who announce it on Facebook.

9
We talk to keep from thinking, drink to keep from drowning, kiss a stranger to keep from tasting the sweet bitters of the one we love.

10
The womb never forgets.

11
The best cure for too much talk? A gently lapping lake—I mean to drown the talker in.

12
Books don't make you smarter, only less tolerant of your own ignorance.

13
Politician: one who has taught himself to shake paws and play dead at the same time.

14
Can you hear the angels singing? Me neither.

15
Full fridge, empty fridge: how these competing pleasures eat at each other!

16
An exiled Polish writer, reading to a packed auditorium of students at noon on a Friday: "This is definitely *not* the hour of poetry."

17
Confess with your whole body, like a robin twitching itself clean in a puddle.

18
The older I get the higher I rise—on the Grim Reaper's to-do list.

19
Astonish the gods: return that borrowed hammer.

Lance Larsen

60. OH! OUR LOVE!

Our love is not a mere physical
that is fleshy like a chubby baby.
Our love is magical, mystical
imbued with charm, beauty, that never
expresses itself in mere, ordinary words.

Our love is a sudden awakening in a dream—
a dream that is within me; no one can
see my beloved lady by lake.

Our love knows no time zones;
our love like a ship of life on the horizon
keeps us misty; yet, as we draw toward
each other, makes us look bigger, sharper,
in all our splendor of stern, starboard, sails.

Our love knows no storms, no tempests;
our ship of love sails smoothly on calm
waters wafted by soothing gentle winds.

Our ship will not call on ports;
our ship will always be on waters
driven by tender and soothing winds of love,
not by tempests of mere passion and envy.

Satyam S. Moorty

61. BLUE SENTINELS

(In memory of my grandmother Lettie Nielsen)

Along the cross-lot path there stood a row
Of sentinels in royal blue. Each held
Its head erect pointing toward a cloud
That stretched like lazy lace and held the glow

Of early summer's dawn. And just as she
Unspokenly had promised year on year –
So like a sibyl from another sphere –
They stoody as though grandmother's prophesy

Was their command. And watching as I passed
She laid her sewing by and joined me there
Beside the pasture fence. No need for prayer
We both knew whom to thank. The dawn had cast

A spell that held us close. Delphiniums
Hold memories to fill melleniums.

Florin R. Nielsen

62. A SINGULAR VERMILION SKY

I touched a snowflake on the windowsill.
Its definition formed a symmetry
That I would hold engraved on memory.
But memory could not retain the thrill
Held in an instant which had disappeared
As quickly as the crystalline beauty.
I saw a sunbeam tease a silent sea
And momentarily, just as I feared,
It too was left to memory. I heard
A whippoorwill in afternoon make moan
And felt it just as though it were my own.
For years I searched with care to find a word
To share a metaphor and found that I
Have known a singular vermilion sky.

Florin R. Nielsen

63. COLORS ON THE HILL

I yearn to see the colors on the hill
In late summer before the chill of Fall.
The flowers' fragrance lingers with me still.

There is peace suffused with a gentle thrill
To stand on Gobbler's Knob, as I recall.
I yearn to see the colors on the hill.

Vermillion Lamb's Ear and Larkspur distill
Rich memories to silently enthrall.
The flowers' fragrance lingers with me still.

The Columbine's yellow and white fulfill,
Rejuvenate as they stand stately tall.
I yearn to see the colors on the hill.

Look up, look down the incline as you will,
You feel as though wrapped in a blessed prayer shawl.
The flowers' fragrance lingers with me still.

Tempted to stand and gaze for hours until
I knew I must descend before nightfall.
I yearn to see the colors on the hill.
The flowers' fragrance lingers with me still.

Florin R. Nielsen

64. THE SILVER LINING OF FISH

An hour of listless fishing
off the pier at Farmington Pond
ends when a stranger
speaks through the smile of dark
enigmatic eyes,
"My name is Angel Rivera,
let me help you."
His caring tone voices
the interest of a brother.

He takes my pole, clips off
the old lure and treble-hooks
a bobbed, gossamer leader--
"Try this my friend, it will
work well for you."

I cast out into deep water.

On a nearby bench
Angel's ill wife waits patiently.
He moves like grace to her,
whispers, comforts a touch
of his hand to her face
she regards with a smile.

The echoing splash of canyon springs
from the east bank fades
into a vision of life beyond the pond--
where there are no more
weeds to pull, nor pain to bear
or loves to leave, and then
a startled tug on the line--
a fish silvers to the surface.

In the blush of early sun
a cloud-dappled sky shimmers
like wings on the water.

Joel Passey

65. OBJET TROUVE

There behind the barn, where they
mowed down the pasture grass, see,
great-grandpa's old wagon --
the wheel spokes splayed from hub sockets,
iron rims, rusted brown.

When new, he hauled timber for the barn,
bales of hay, sacks of grain, barrels,
dry goods and firewood to homesteads
down south from Fillmore.

Took his boys along with him for help
when it was freighted up. Slept under it
at night or rested in its shade on desert treks.

Generations of riding boots
have scuffed away the floorboards;
the bolster seat, flattened and gray
except where it tucks into seams.

The back gear has wobbled out of line--
like heavy loads carried long on a spine.

Harness traces, still fastened to the singletree
molder in the sod.

> Remember grandma telling us how it was decked with wild
> roses and sunflowers as part of Hazel's wedding train?

Visible in the warped, wagon bed planks
the outline of old blood
from that horse kick splintered leg.

> *Hyrum would have bled to death, ma said,*
> *if it hadn't been for a Ezra*
> *who tied him off*
> *and hauled him in to town.*

Winter freeze has cracked the brake block in two.
The hitch and end-gate rod have lost their useful shine.

The flutter of a yellow breasted meadowlark
perches on the side panel, to warble the passing time.

Joel Passey

66. MEMORIES OF LONG AGO

remembering past times of long ago,
prairies, seasons, hardships, love,
looking now beyond the darkened chimney
standing there among fallen walls,
all that is left of the homestead house
bringing memories of years past
watching rainbow colored wild flowers flutter in the wind,
memories of chicken coops, a rooster announcing the sunrise
miles of barbed wire fence some posts stand tall while,
others bent with age and weather fall upon the ground
looking further across the land, seeing if only in the minds eye,
hay with haystacks so tall, gardens growing for harvesting
smells blending, mixing silently together,
building nostalgic memories of special things
like homemade bread cooking in the oven
and root beer bubbling from cast iron pots
walking down paths of the fallen homestead,
seeing not just a pile of rubble all around
but memories from births to deaths all are there
promises, heartaches. hard work, happiness, sadness,
memories remain there forever among the debris,
knowing that life is not an exaggeration of the past
just wonderful memories building a future.

Gail Peterson

67. COAST TO COAST

Determination to link the nation coast to coast
led those stalwart souls building a steel highway
for the transcontinental, reaching from east to west
rails laid upon the ties as hammers met the spikes
one at a time, on down the line,
under conditions not of their making
with desert winds whistling free,
blowing, swirling, dust, bringing exhausting heat
followed by torrents of rain
until freezing cold ushered in hard, winter blizzards
when all elements of nature worked to discourage
the meeting of the rails, finishing of the transcontinental
determination prevailed, hour by hour, day by day
until the last rail was laid in place
across the prairie coal smoke rose skyward
across mountain ranges smoke and noises came
as the trains coming east to west and west to east
met at Promontory Point where a golden spike welded forever
the meeting of the rails.................coast to coast

Gail Peterson

68. BRAVE PIONEER WOMEN

a humble soul bearing her load with faith
journeyed to a remote almost savage land
crossing endless plains and mountains
fighting bitter winds, rain, and snow
shallow graves dot hillsides and prairies
where brave souls met their journeys end
to illness, childbirth, Indians and more
sometimes the journey seemed to much
a path of sorrow and uncertainty
swirled in dust, measured in pain,
where she put her trust in God
leaving behind religion persecution
traveling in fear and tears, memories
made from yesterdays realities
leaving tracks of blood behind
where broken trails woven together
from wagon wheels turning and
handcarts following along
her inner strength was drawn from
pathways dug deep, from yesterdays struggles
this pioneer woman with faith so high
courage so brave, working so hard
enduring a life of sacrifice
awaiting the end of the enduring journey
when "All Is Well" rings loud and clear

Gail Peterson

69. NEAR MOAB

I hiked an arch,
a walkway through the sky,
lunched high in the edgy shade
beneath the sandstone bridge,
a gift of the wind.

Patricia Peterson

70. DRIPPING HOURS FLOW

As I hike up the dusty trail
to Diamond Fork Hot Springs,
Rich and Nick beside me.
We pass the wooden sign:
Warning —Possible nude bathers.
Sego lilies and sagebrush wander
the hillsides.

A hot spring gushes
from the middle of the mud
in a cache near the mountain's ridge.
We, with other younger bathers,
splash and soak on logs in the brownish water.
As the afternoon shadows wade
into the hot pool,
a gray, diamond-back, boa-sized
blow snake slithers
toward us.

The youth squeal and gather rocks,
start stoning the ancient snake.
No! I shout, leaping
between them and the snake.
This old snake is harmless!
Snake decides he's not charmed,
crawls back into his dark crevice.
Who knew I am protector of snakes?

Patricia Peterson

71. MARY'S REVERIE

Memories swirl in Mary's mind
some bitter as the winds of bigotry
that drove them from home
into brutal exodus across the frozen Mississippi.

Widow, two daughters and son
bend into buffeting storm,
fight for each forward footstep, finding
abandoned, broken-down log hut
for their night's refuge.

Midst increased gales and leaky roof,
sleep eludes Mary and sensing something wrong,
finds mother lying still, too cold.

Would the night ever end?
Mary and Kathryn cling, cry, console,
and try to quiet little Henry —
a tall order for children braving the
greatest trial of a lifetime.
Daylight brings help
in the form of the kind and heavy-laden.
Three orphans are divided.

Wretched memories, numbed by grief and hardship,
rouse reluctantly of Henry's body being lowered
into final resting place at Winter Quarters;
scurvy's a fancy name for starvation.

But her last recollection is pleasant —
she walks the banks of immigrant-encamped creek
and stumbles by chance upon little sister Kathryn.

Not much left of once proud family
but two young sisters embrace with
all the joy of love and living —
a memory to cling to, indeed.

Susan Randall

72. I WILL BE "TIL I DIE

As aged, worn and faded as Grandma herself,
lay newspaper clippings atop her garage shelf.
Selected and stacked with deliberate care
a half-century of history headlines were there.

When she died family found, sorting through her possessions,
these journalistic gems that left quite an impression.
There was John F. Kennedy's assassination,
presidential election results of our nation,
communism's menace, it's failure and fall,
the miraculous leveling of the Berlin wall,
deaths of world-wide beloved church heads,
the heralding in of those put in their stead,
catastrophies, calamities, intrigues and wars,
and the small step on moon mankind leaped to explore.

Amidst these sensations, was one that brought grins —
a football score headline after years of no wins
'gainst an in-state rival, and a "Ute" through and through,
she'd tallied with her treasures, "Utah Beats B.Y.U."

Susan Randall

73. WE, DESERT DWELLERS

Fierce overflows of
the flash-flooded wash
leave beauty behind
and solace.

Inside red quiet
we, too, strip down
to the curve of the land:
savor this exuberance of sparsity

Susan Roche

74. BEES AFTER SCORPION

I wrap the scorpion just so,
in case of later side effects,
shake out sheets, inspect sills,
and wonder why I don't just drive away.

Instead, in the morning,
I park myself on the porch
close to the husky thrum of floating bees
that sip from the sunflowers' dark hearts
and drift back into purple blooms
whose names I can't yet say.

Their murmur meanders like a
didgeridoo, primeval and low, while I,
harmonizing deep in my throat,
rest inside their rumble.

I begin to learn where I am.

Susan Roche

75. PERFORMING MYSELF IN THE CITY
WHERE I LIVED BEFORE

You glide near me, my shadow side, my
city self, your eyes no longer easy
to read. I stretch to pull you close, we hold
hands, I remember you. We have always
laughed a lot.

When you jerk me forward, my wrist
begins to ache. I stumble, squint: so much
sparkle, too much pulse.
You drag me all over. 'Come on...come
ON' - all this talking.

You remember their stories, avid
for chapters you have missed, but when they
begin to catch up with you, your throat
swells, your edges
fray, there are pauses.

You try to perform the I who was before
but that old script has faded.

When you decide to let me speak,
I whisper 'well, you know, in the desert...'

SAND and SKY: Poems from Utah

They smile fondly.
I start again: 'I never knew the tips of junipers...'
Smiles, on timers, waver.

I flicker next to you but drop your hand,
ready now to leave you
in the performance space of other minds,
while I return to light that learns new colors,
to a quiet thick as blood.

Susan Roche

76. A MEETING

Arches National Park

here where the river flooded and wore
through Jurassic rock a channel

we reconsider   empty
from Old English *aemettig* (at leisure)

the "p" a euphonic addition
language and leisure filled

to help us make sense of our senses
as now when in red sand with a dusting of snow

I see the print of my boots
hear the thrum of salt thousands of feet thick

smell sunlight like carbonation in the air
empty of smog here

where the stream doesn't have to be here
                        to be felt

Natasha Sajé

77. KRISTALLNACHT

The night she left us last,
I awoke to broken glass.
My father was showing me,
But didn't tell me
His heart had fallen apart.
So picture frames and store bought art
Littered the patch of concrete
That I came upon – discrete.
Who has done this? Destroyed our pictures!
I swept up the glass & trashed the bitter,
And nobody but me, cleaned
The broken glass in the sun gleamed,
And only I guarded photos of family
Like a dragon,
In a trove,
But no gold,
Just bits of glass and bits of me.
My parent's marriage was glass--
My home turned to frames needing repair.
The night she left us last
I never thought I would share
My night of broken glass, my Kristallnacht,
A sad shadow's reign,
My night of broken glass, my Kristallnacht,
Cheeks streaked with human rain.

Eva Sanchez

78. THE GIRL LOST IN TIME

You wear
30's glasses and owl rimmed as you are
You creature in the dark are lost in space
You don't know what time you are

The sound barely breathing
Didn't know boots gnarled from 90's could
Be SO QUIET
So I listen
And you speak of the time you traveled
In a car, 80 mph so fast you actually found
The track of time

I let it go and cringe and cry and complain
Your lips dry, cracked, red droplets forming again.
You scream for a time traveler to take you back

But no lamp to be rubbed appears
Only the memories of the man you most feared
Whose smell and taste and dark eyes leer
And come back to you like the vintage dress of
A grandmother long gone who didn't notice
Baby is getting hurt in the guest room again

You vomit the past and swallow the traces
That will stay with you forever
His ghost constantly beating and living and never
Passing on
Make new memories with me
Make new words with me
Forget the ones he told you

Now I'm not telling you time heals all wounds
Because it only heals some
I'm telling you to take what he didn't break
And run, baby run

Eva Sanchez

79. SIPAPU

A poem left at Perfect Kiva on the last solar eclipse

My place is the space
between two deserts,
one made of red sandstone,
where in each Sego Lily
I see turlough[1] violets. The other
is made of grey limestone, where
beneath each Blackthorn tree
I smell the sweet smoke
of burning Juniper. In that space I hear
the Canyon Wren in the Lapwing's weep,
and the crannogs[2] I circle become kivas.
My place is here, and there,
where I know the veil between this world
and the other is thin, where rocks speak
of the Anasazi or the Tuatha De Danann,
and where memories stir from a sipapu within,
bidding me to leave one place for the other.

Meghan Nuttall Sayres

1. A turlough is a sudden pool created by a rise of the water table in the limestone "deserts" of Western Ireland.
2. A crannog is an ancient, circular dwelling in Ireland.

80. A MOUNTAIN IN THE NORTH

There is a lofty mountain in the north
    and a temple – the only shelter –
    on the mountain summit.
Those who go to the temple to pray stay there
    to relax and to rejoice.
"They have no speech, they use no words." [*Psalm*, 19:3]
The mountain air is filled with naked meanings
    and pure understanding.
That is how they pray on that mountain.

We can climb the mountain because there is a climber in us.
Many wish to go to that mountain in the north,
    but no map will locate it on Earth.
Only the North Star guides the wayfarers.
And as one walks to seek it a pathway appears.
It is said that there are as many pathways to the mountain top
    as the number of the wayfarers.
"Who may truly ascend the sacred mountain?"
"The one who has clean hands and a pure heart." [*Psalm*, 24: 3-4]

What we know of the mountain and its inhabitants
    come from brief poems inscribed on pebbles and gemstones
    that pilgrims bring back as souvenirs.
Rivers also carry the magical pebbles down to our earth.
"These gemstones," the pilgrims report, "are made of light
    up in the mountain, but as they are brought down,
    they crystalize into beautiful shapes and brilliant colors
    and reveal hidden messages and good news,
    all of which were unspoken but lived
    by the mountain inhabitants."

Grandparents walking with their grandchildren
    along creeks and river banks
    sometimes find these rock crystals.
"Children" they say, "are better at finding them, but grandparents are better at reading them."

It is also said that the gemstones shine more brilliantly at night,
    and if you get hold of a few of these pebbles
    you can walk through the darkest valleys of life:
"You will not fear the terror of night." [*Psalm*, 91: 5]

Poems on Pebbles: A Random Harvest

An old man of the mountain once gave twelve gemstones to a group of hikers and the following poems were inscribed on them:

Every day is Thanksgiving.
True happiness is an outcome of compassionate service.
You can know truth only when you are real.
Birth, life and death all come from love.
Life is a gift, so can be death.
Yesterday never exists and tomorrow always comes as today.
If life does not pass, everyone dies.
One can live only here and now – nowhere else, no other time.
No creature is immortal and yet everyone is eternal.
Trust in God and do you work lovingly; do not be attached to rewards.
Love handles everything.
The fish gently swims on the moon while the moon lies still on the lake.

Rasoul Shams

81. IRONY

Mountains hard, unyielding,
absorbing noon-day heat,
scored with cracks and crevices-
providing hand-holds
for searching fingers.

Climbers, tiny temporal beings,
trying to match wits with
these eternal peaks
reaching
far into the sky.

A fly on the wall,
a temporary nuisance
not worth noticing are these
small beings
with such intrusive hardware.

Long after these climbers
are old men with
memories of seconds of glory
will these
mountains still stand.

Men cannot even begin to scar
these craggy surfaces:
but water and wind -
drop by drop, breath by breath,
can reduce these mounts to grains of sand.

Carolyn W. Taylor

82. BIRDSONG

A flush of finches fill the sky
pale pink
spark of silver
a rippling flock with one voice
the sound of light
breath bursting

Let the day begin
Let birds save us

One tanager swoops tree to tree
gold and orange
black-winged
silent

frogs chirp at dusk
and swallows dive
catching insects

Do not risk joy
Let joy besiege you

Everything loves life:
bird, child, fish, mosquito—
you hear the fluttery
whoosh
of your own heart

Let your body rise
Let the wind blow through you

SAND and SKY: Poems from Utah

Beautiful, you are
the whole world here:
wings, stone, water, twilight
song and the end of song
dark in the dark
leaves trembling

Hush now, sweet child:
Isn't the breath you share with birds holy?

Melanie Rae Thon

83. FOR A DEAD FAWN ON THE HIGHWAY

There was a gentleness in your going down,
a beauty, too, never held
by those empowered ones
who flail the world
but also wither down
in the wake of some dying sun.
Now you'll never know
the terror of the hunt,
so be always an innocence of nature
which copper leaves need never hide
from threatening vistas,
careless trodders,
and rumbling caravans,
who'll surely fly you by into some oblivion.
A gentle thing never suspects its nearness
to the roots of heaven.
Be sheltered now
by the high leaves of silver spring
which rustle
then sing,
bearing witness
to your holy death.

Howard N. Tuttle

84. DAS HEILIGE

(After Psalm 72: The mountains shall bring peace to the people)

Above the grey valley,
the city of stones,
stand the hills,
which seem to speak
an everlastingness.

In ancient Greece poets preceded the priest,
and even now poets may remind us
the flatlands are not the landscape of the soul.

A dwelling place remains,
up, up where the air is pure,
steadying the mind
which remembers the mountains too have suffered,
yet stand.

May the mountains recall us
from the futility of things
without law, meaning, or end,
from the stockpiling of sand,
the melted trivia of lives,
the distractions that make us forget
we are still enduring to be free.

SAND and SKY: Poems from Utah

Above the twilight of the plains,
the valley of shadows,
teach us thanks,
the deeper heart,
the higher range,
the Holy.

Howard N. Tuttle

85. FLY

Edges and ledges
empty skies and desert plains
sand shifts
six days of ceaseless winds

upon cracked and broken
lips...yesterday's kiss
lingers on
spilling love sounds
across a tussled spoiled night

off beyond the bouldered bluff
young coyotes crying wolf
a sudden silent shout
pierces arid ears
blusters by
motherless
nests of baby birds
perched past reach
of upstretched arms

lunar light
strikes shadows on
stolen miles
old men with sickly smiles
dance to off key tune
drunk in the gloom
of dark land's plight

an elder
strains to hear
a tiny utter rising
below the sound of dawn

hope, give them hope
let go wild wind
wild wind, let go
Let Go
this land is ours
let go a shout
LET GO our land
her future is our fortune,
Let us reap not rape her
Release your grip and LET HER FLY!

Linda Waters

86. SAND AND SKY

silent sand cloaked
in seven shades of red
 sun-soaks a shadowed
downward slope

sandstone silhouettes
shyly gaze
donning waves
of auburn surf

sunken sun sheds
her desert skirt
at skies edge as
sheets of stars
summon a single moth

she flits sand to rock
strands of glitter
strung across a swollen night

she vanishes in a twinkle
swallowed by summer's
half lit cobalt sky

skin of naked moonrise
wears her sideways crescent smile

sandman draws his somber blinds
 in soulful slumber Summer lies

Linda Waters

STATE SYMBOLS

The following are state symbols of Utah. Is this a poem? Yes, as far as poetry is essentially a set of symbols and their meanings.

State Animal:	Rocky Mountain Elk
State Bird:	California Seagull
State Cooking Pot:	Dutch Oven
State Emblem:	Beehive
State Fish:	Bonneville Cutthroat Trout
State Flower:	Sego Lily
State Folk Dance:	Square Dance
State Fossil:	Allosaurus
State Fruit:	Cherry
State Gem:	Topaz
State Grass:	Indian Rice Grass
State Insect:	Honey Bee
State Mineral:	Copper

State Motto:	"Industry"
State Rock:	Coal
State Song:	"Utah, This Is The Place"
State Hymn:	"Utah We Love Thee"
State Star:	Dubhe
State Tree:	Quaking Aspen
State Vegetable:	Spanish Sweet Onion
State Historic Vegetable:	Sugar Beet
State Winter Sports:	Skiing and Snowboarding
State Astronomical Symbol:	Beehive Cluster located in the constellation of Cancer the Crab.
State Firearm:	John M. Browning designed M1911 automatic pistol
State Railroad Museum:	Ogden Union Station

SHORT BIOGRAPHIES OF CONTRIBUTORS

Margo Andrews is a native of Utah and a graduate of the University of Utah's Department of Theatre's Actor Training Program. Additionally, she trained at the American Conservatory Theatre in San Francisco, CA, and Trinity Repertory Conservatory in Providence, RI. Margo's professional acting career includes over 20 years of experience in stage work, television, and film. With five national tours to her credit, she has performed in 48 states. Her commercial and industrial film credits include work for such companies and organizations as Target, Ford Motors, USSB Television, 3M, The Minnesota Orchestra, and Dayton Hudson, to name a few. A lover of poetry and drama, Margo Andrews is a professor in the University of Utah's Department of Theatre.

Roger Evans Baker. A Utah grad student couple brought Roger Evans Baker into the world while living in São Paulo, Brazil, in 1964. Nelson and Lucille reared Roger and his five siblings in East Brunswick, New Jersey. Following a second stint in Brazil and one in Portugal, Roger earned his BA in English at Brigham Young University, along with a minor in Portuguese. There his professors sowed the seeds of a love of poetry. Following law school at BYU, Roger returned to Portugal to study international law as a Fulbright scholar. In 1993 Roger went to work as a criminal prosecutor for Tooele City, Utah, where in 1995 the Mayor and City Council appointed him to the position of City Attorney. He continues to work there today. Father of seven children, Roger, in his free time, raises chickens, walks Erda's farm-flanked roads, reads, and occasionally writes poetry. Roger's most recent project is the book *Rabbit Lane: Memoir of a Country Road* (2016).

Vera Ogden Bakker has lived in Utah for all of her 84 years. She graduated from Utah State University and taught elementary school in Utah for 25 years. She has published several children's books and a book of poetry. Vera lives in West Bountiful, Utah, and loves visits from her five children, 11 grandchildren, 13 great-grand-children, and many friends. She loves children, books, and poetry. She is a member of the Utah State Poetry Society.

Marilyn L. Ball was born on a cattle ranch in Roosevelt, Utah in 1929, a big surprise to older parents, while business men in NY were leaping off tall buildings due to the demise of money. Educated as a nurse at the University of Utah, she loved her nursing career, raising a beloved family, enjoying cabin, skiing, and traveling. All the while, in her self-taught way, writing poetry, up to this day. She is thankful to the Utah State Poetry Society and the League of Utah Writers for their invaluable help.

Shanan Ballam teaches poetry writing, fiction writing, and composition at Utah State University in Logan. She is the author of the chapbook *The Red Riding Hood Papers* (Finishing Line, 2010) and the full-length poetry collection *Pretty Marrow* (Negative Capability, 2013) which was a semi-finalist for the 2010 Brittingham and Polk Poetry Prizes, the 2010 May Swenson Award, the 2010 Philip Levine Prize in Poetry, and the 2012 Louise Bogan Award; in 2012 it received first place in the Utah Arts Council's Original Writing Contest, judged by Sue Walker, former Poet Laureate of Alabama. In 2013, she was appointed to the Utah Arts Council Board of Directors.

Cindy Bechtold is a busy grandmother, tending her three-year-old grandson four days a week. She's past president of both "Word Weavers" and "Write On," two Utah State Poetry Society groups. She placed in the annual L.D.S. music and arts poetry contest several seasons and has a children's story published in the *Friend* magazine. Her poetry can also be found in *Golden Words*, *For Poets Fifty and Older*, and in *Panorama* (an annual publication by the Utah State Poetry Society). Her poetry chapbook *Polished Edges* was published in 2011 by the American Fork Arts Council.

Neil Bowen is 61 and lives in Kamas, Utah. He works in Salt Lake and surrounding areas in the gas and oil business. A member of the Utah State Poetry Society, Neil has written numerous poems. He and his wife Karen are in a second marriage and have 20 grandchildren together.

Doug Brewer was a "full time cowboy growin' up" on ranches near Bear Lake where he drank in ranch hand banter and yarn-spinning, fodder for his growing penchant for poetry. He claims his works are 5% serious and 98% not. He loves writing and the art of performance. He has been President of Babcock Performing Readers, on the Board of Cowboy Poets of Utah, has received BSA's Silver Antelope and the Purple Heart and Bronze Star for Meritorious Service in Vietnam. He and Linda live in Holladay and have eight children, "all girls but seven."

Markay Brown was born in Idaho and raised in Seattle. She graduated from BYU where she later worked as an admissions officer. Following retirement, she began writing poetry. She won first place for her manuscript, *Eve's Child*, in the 2014 Utah Original Writing Competition, Book-length collection of Poetry, judged by Richard Howard of Columbia University. Her poems have appeared in *Segullah*, *Provo/Orem Word*, *15 Bytes*, *Encore*, *Southern Quill*, and elsewhere. She is mother of five sons and grandmother of 13. Family, friends, reading, writing, music, and long walks in the red rocks make her happy. She resides in St. George, Utah.

Marleen Bussma has been a cowgirl at heart since growing up with horses and cows on a small North Dakota farm. Her poems include stories about her rural life and her interest in the old West. Her writing has earned the 2016 Cowboy Poetry Book of the Year Award and the Will Rogers Medallion Award for excellence in western literature. She has performed at various venues in Arizona, Nevada, Utah, all the way up to North Dakota. She is an invited performer to the National Cowboy Poetry Gathering in Elko, Nevada. She is retired and lives with her husband Vaughn in Dammeron Valley, Utah.

D. Gary Christian was born in Portland, Oregon in 1929. He grew up in Raymond, Alberta, Canada and returned to United States sometime thereafter to serve in the U. S Army from 1947-1950. He attended BYU from 1953-1956 and the University of Utah School of Law from 1956-1959. He practiced law for 37 years in Salt Lake City, and retired in 1996. He presently lives in Santa Clara, Utah where he writes poetry.

Tyler Clark is a poet from Monterey, California who currently resides in Provo, Utah. His poetry has been published in *Touchstones* and *Inspired: A Community Poetry Writing Experience*. He finds inspiration from scuba diving into life and overturning rocks at the ocean floor. And he loves Italian food.

Anastasia M. Clarke lives in Orem, UT. She moved to Utah from Florida about four years ago and spends most her spare time writing poems.

Brock Dethier directs the composition program at Utah State University and writes books for composition students and teachers, most recently, *21 Genres and How to Write Them*. He has published a poetry chapbook, *Ancestor Worship*, and in 2015 Popcorn Press published his first full-length book of poems, *Reclamation*.

Stacy W. Dixon loves how the written word connects us through time and place. Her work has appeared in *The Mid-America Poetry Review, Tiger's Eye, Blood Lotus, Pirene's Fountain, Sweet Tree Review* and has been nominated for a Pushcart Prize. Her chapbook collection *A Pebble Thrown in Water* was published by Tiger's Eye Press. She lives in Utah with her husband and three sons.

Fae Ellsworth was raised in a bookish family in Berkeley, California, where her parents paid their children to memorize poetry. As a word lover, she graduated with a B.A. in English, with a creative writing emphasis from Brigham Young University, raised a family, and at age 50 earned an MFA in ceramics and sculpture from the same university. She lives, writes, and creates art in the Virgin Utah desert home which she and her sculptor husband Brent Gehring built with their own hands. She relies regularly on Rumi as a source of inspiration, truth, and enlightenment.

Lin Vernon Floyd, a retired school librarian, resides in St. George, Utah. Active with the Utah State Poetry Society as Chapters Coordinator and President of Dixie Poets, she chairs the annual Poetry in the Park held in Zion Park each spring, and started the Youth Poetry Contest for Washington County School District. Former columnist for the *Senior Sampler*, she has published several books: *Looking Back, Find Your Voice-Write Your Life Story* and *Nature Notes for Kids* – a collection of children's poems that placed second in the Utah State Division of Arts and Museums' 2010 contest for juvenile books.

Bonnie Glee (aka Bonnie Glee Speth Thomas) is a Utah writer who lives in Cottonwood Heights, the city between the canyons. She has published poetry, short stories, newspaper profiles, magazine articles, and three literary novels: *Satine Murder* (2014), *Token Woman* (2015), and *Invisible Son* (2016). She's been a long time member of the League of Utah Writers and the Utah State Poetry Society. She is retired from the business world and enjoys everyday with retired hubby, Joe, their children, grandchildren, great-grandchildren, and of course writing.

Lynne H. Goodhart was born in Salt Lake City. At age 17, she went to live in France for the summer on an American Field Service scholarship. This led her to being a French major at the University of Utah; upon graduation, she was awarded a Fulbright scholarship to France, then to the University of Colorado at Boulder majoring in French. After earning a Ph.D. there in 1972, she worked first at the

University of Wisconsin - La Crosse and then at Utah State University in Logan, teaching French language and literature. She was editor of the Poetry section of the annual student magazine at East High School in Salt Lake City. She has published (with co-author Jon Wagner) a book of translations of the poetry of Andrée Chedid (Fugitive Suns), one of France's most popular woman poets. She became interested in Rumi's poetry in the 1990s and is working on a book titled "Conversations with Rumi." After retiring from Utah State University, Professor Lynne Goodhart still resides in Logan where she volunteers as a tutor at the English Language Center.

Sylvia Ruth Gray is retired from years of employment as a medical transcriptionist. She owns and manages rental property on The Avenues (where she has lived for over three decades). She has two daughters, four grandkids, as well as cats, raccoons, and hundreds of rock doves. She has followed a grain-based diet as a spiritual discipline since 1983 and enjoys a sturdy reputation for vegan cooking and teaching. In 2016, her booklet, *EATING ANIMALS: Would George Ohsawa and Michio Kushi Be Vegan Today*, was published by the non-profit press, Planetary Health, Inc. She has also published poems in the USA and overseas.

Dawnell Hatton Griffin was born in Millard County, Utah, the youngest of seven children. At an early age she was interested in becoming a writer. As an adult, she has written prize-winning poetry, short stories, children's stories and family histories. She was selected as the Utah Poet of the Year in 2012 by the Utah State Poetry Society for her winning book *On Judgment Day*. She served as president of the Utah State Poetry Society in 2015-2016.

Maurine Haltiner taught high school English for 33 years in Salt Lake City. She was Utah State Poetry Society Poet of the Year in 2004 for her winning poetry book *A Season and A Time*. She has served as editor of the UTSPS annual poetry journal *Panorama*. She has also published a young adult novel titled *Truth Windows*. She is principal 2nd violin in the Wasatch Community Symphony Orchestra.

Lindsay Jane Hanks was born in the mountains of rural New Mexico and has called various points along the Rockies her home. She currently resides in Salt Lake City where she can be found climbing in the mountains, reading in the library, running in the hills, writing in her journal, skiing in the backcountry, and seeking a life purpose.

Alina Hansen is a student at the University of Utah majoring in English. Her poem 'La Recette' was published in the University of Utah's literary journal *The Canticle* (2016).

Rebecca Holt studied at Brigham Young University, obtained a Master's degree in clinical psychology Santa Barbara Graduate Institute, and has trained in energy medicine with Alberto Villoldo and The Four Winds Society, RYT 200, Masters NLP Certification (Neuro-Linguistic Programming) and sound vibration healing. Based in Salt Lake City, she provides Sound Weaving workshops for varied groups such as health and wellness, and creativity retreats and conferences, yoga retreats and classes, and private and corporate events. Rebecca's work with sound and its impact on human experience has been featured at creative conferences and workshops around the world, including recently with noted poet David Whyte, a series of women's movement retreats from Bali, Indonesia to Kauai as well as for the Wellness Collective at the 2017 Sundance Film Festival.

Lorraine Jeffery earned her bachelor's degree in English and her master's degree in library science, and managed public libraries in Texas, Ohio and Utah for over 20 years. She has won poetry prizes in state and national contests and has published over 50 poems in various publications, including *Clockhouse, Kindred, Calliope, Ibbetson Street,* and *Rockhurst Review*. She has published short stories in *Elsewhere, War Cry, The Standard* and *Persimmon Tree*. Her articles have appeared in *Focus on the Family, Mature Years, and Utah's Senior Review*, as well as other publications. Her first mystery novel was released in May of 2015. She is the mother of 10 children (eight adopted) and lives with her husband in Orem, Utah.

Grace Diane Jessen is a life-long resident of Utah. She is a member of the League of Utah Writers and the Utah State Poetry Society. She is primarily a poet, but also enjoys writing histories, essays, and stories. She lives in Glenwood, Utah, with her husband, Gordon.

George King was born in Spanish Fork, Utah and worked summers on his grandfather's farm. He married Sharon McRae from American Fork and lived in Orem until her death. He has since married Gayanne Ramsden, also from Orem.

Gayanne & George are now living happily ever after in Orem, Utah. George King has taught French and English at BYU, Utah Valley University, and Rice University in Utah. He and Gayanne have five children and 16 grandchildren. "We love Utah and the wonderful life it offers us."

Kate Kirkham is from Salt Lake City. After graduating from the University of Utah, she worked in Washington DC for 11 years. She returned to Utah to be on the faculty of the Marriott School of Management, BYU. Now retired she continues to think about organizational change and diversity – with more time for poetry

Marjorie Kyriopoulos grew up as a member of a big fat Greek family in Salt Lake City, Utah and relocated to the Twin Cities in 1989. She has been a writer all her life—personally and professionally. While living in Utah, she raised two children, a son and daughter, who are now adults. She was a member of the Editorial Board for *Network Magazine*, a women's publication. Some of her poems were published in that magazine during the 1970s. Photography and writing are her two passions in life. For more information visit www.shutterandpen.com

Lance Larsen, Poet Laureate of Utah (2012-2017), has published four poetry collections, most recently *Genius Loci* (Tampa, 2013). He has received a number of awards, including a Pushcart Prize and a fellowship from the National Endowment for the Arts. He teaches at BYU and in spring 2017 will co-direct a study abroad program in London. He is married to Jacqui Larsen, a painter and collage artist. Their teenage daughter, Tessa, is quite sure she wants to be a chemist.

Satyam Sikha Moorty (S.S. Moorty). Originally from India, Moorty did his PhD in American literature from the University of Utah, Salt Lake City, and taught for 31 years at Southern Utah University, Cedar City, Utah, courses such as F. Scott Fitzgerald, Shakespeare, and Eastern Literatures in English translation. He was a Fulbright professor in Yemen, Moldova (thrice), Austria, and Azerbaijan, a Balkan Scholar at the American University in Bulgaria. He has published scholarly articles as well as poetry in the USA, UK, Canada, India, France, Spain, South Africa, Romania, Moldova, Azerbaijan, and Ukraine. He is also the author of a book of poems and short stories titled *Distant Lands, Diverse Cultures*. Now retired, he pursues this passion of writing poetry.

Florin Nielsen was born in 1931 in the town of Hyde Park in northern Utah. At 19, he went to the Netherlands as a missionary. After graduation from Utah State University in Logan, he served at the US Air Force for two-and-half years. Mr. Nielsen has a long and distinguished career of service in Utah in the fields of drama, English literature, public education and various arts committees and community activities. He taught at East High School for 25 years; he has also taught poetry classes for senior citizens for a number of years. He lives in Salt Lake City and has a daughter, a son, and seven grandchildren. As he once said, "A book, a pen, his family and friends are his comfort and muse."

Joel Passey is a long-time member of the Utah State Poetry Society (UTSPS) and served as UTSPS president from 2001-2003. He served as reader for the UTSPS-sponsored Youth Category Contest. He is currently active in the UTSPS-Ben Lomond Chapter. He is a retired associate professor of communication from Weber State University. He and his wife Florence reside in Layton, Utah.

Gail M Peterson is a member of the Ben Lomond Poets, and the Utah State Poetry Society. She has been writing for about all her life. Some of her poems have been published and some have won awards in Utah. She studied at the University of Utah and Weber State University. She lives in Roy, Utah, has three children, six grandchildren and two great grandchildren.

Patricia Peterson is a lover of life in the Rockies, former English instructor, publisher of one book (*Canandaigua to Carthage*, 2007), mother of seven, grandmother of 18, and awakes with anticipation and curiosity each morning to view the changing grandeur of Earth and Sky.

Susan Randall is a member of Word Weavers (Provo, Utah) and the Utah State Poetry Society. She has entered the state contests, the American Fork "Utah Voices", and the LDS Cultural Arts contests, and has received awards and had poetry published in the books resulting from these competitions. She received her B.A. from the University of Utah, is married to Boyd Randall, has five married daughters, 21 grandchildren and two great grandchildren. She took up piano a few years ago and is still trying to figure it out. It may take the rest of her life.

Susan Roche. After visiting the red rock desert for years, Susan Roche finally realized she could live in no other space. In 2012, she moved from the Washington DC area to the splendor of Castle Valley, a tiny town in southeast Utah. She loves the paradox of poetry: sliding on a poem's words into the word-less places of full attention, floating beneath words, where everything lives.

Natasha Sajé is professor of English at Westminster College in Salt Lake City and a faculty member at the Vermont College of Fine Arts MFA in Writing Program. She is the author of three books of poems, *Red Under the Skin, Bend,* and *Vivarium,* and a book of poetry criticism, *Windows and Doors: A Poet Reads Literary Theory* as well as many essays. For more information on her work visit: www.natashasaje.com

Eva Sanchez was born in California but grew up in southern Utah. With a strong calling to not only nature but the nature of people, Eva has been drawn to expressing herself best through her writing and poetry.

Meghan Nuttall Sayres' latest books of fiction and nonfiction are *Night Letter,* and *Love and Pomegranates: Artists and Wayfarers on Iran.* Her novel *Anahita's Woven Riddle* has been translated into several European and Middle Eastern languages. She is at work on a project *Streetwise Istanbul,* an East-West perspective glimpsing into hearts and minds of our Near Eastern neighbors, featuring weekly words and images from abroad on Facebook and Instagram. A former resident of Utah, she currently lives in Washington State.

Rasoul Shams, PhD in geology, has lived in Iran, India, Japan, and the USA. He founded the Rumi Poetry Club in 2007 on the occasion of the 800th anniversary of Rumi. He has published numerous articles and two books on Rumi: *Rumi: The Art of Loving* (2012) and *Rumi Essays* (2016). He is a proud member of the Utah State Poetry Society.

Carolyn W. Taylor is a member of Utah State Poetry Society (Valley Winds Chapter), and lives in Salt Lake City. Most of her poetry is related to nature. She has a passion for astronomy and for the Utah desert systems. She has been a science teacher and has enjoyed hiking around the world. The Taylor family have a genetic propensity for skiing in Utah's gorgeous mountains.

Melanie Rae Thon is originally from Montana and lives in Salt Lake City, where she teaches in the Creative Writing and Environmental Humanities programs at the University of Utah. Her most recent books are *Silence & Song, The 7th Man,* and *The Good Samaritan Speaks.* She is a recipient of a Fellowship in Creative

Arts from The John Simon Guggenheim Memorial Foundation, a Whiting Writer's Award, the Hopwood Award, two Fellowships from the National Endowment for the Arts, and a Writer's Residency from the Lannan Foundation. In 2009, she was Virgil C. Aldrich Fellow at the Tanner Humanities Center.

Howard Nelson Tuttle, from Salt Lake City, earned his BA and MA from the University of Utah, an M.A. in government from Harvard University, and PhD in the history of philosophy from Brandeis University in 1967. He was professor of philosophy at the University of New Mexico until retirement in 1996. An emeritus professor of philosophy at the University of Utah, he is the author of several books on philosophy. He lives in Salt Lake City with his wife Carolyn, and has two children, Carl (an astrophysicist) and Laura (a child psychiatrist), and granddaughters Emily and Katherine. Howard enjoys writing poems, hiking, skiing, and traveling.

Linda Waters. For many decades, Linda has rambled through unchartered Utah wilderness and left grooves on familiar footworn trails. She has delighted in guiding foreign visitors on spirit walks through pristine wilderness, hoping to soothe their urbanized nature-starved souls. After shedding the cloak of being a cog in the Corporate wheel, she is now free to contribute by being a guide for individuals learning to navigate life's uncharted trails. The wild, raw beauty of Utah awakens the protectionist, Mama Bear determination in her. Her passions are helping preserve Earth's splendid treasures for our children's children, and contributing to creating a more peaceful, just, sane and sustainable world.

ABOUT THIS BOOK

Sand and Sky: Poems from Utah is an anthology of poems contributed by poets from Utah. The volume shares a sense of place, time, and people in the American west. The serif font used for the text of this book is Times New Roman, originally designed by Victor Lardent for the British newspaper *The Times* in 1931. Although no longer used by *The Times*, it is one of most popular typefaces in printing.

ABOUT THE PUBLISHER

RUMI PUBLICATIONS is an imprint of the Rumi Poetry Club, founded in 2007 on the occasion of the eight hundredth anniversary of Rumi's birth in order to foster literature and art that nourish the human spiritual life and enrich our global culture. We celebrate inspirational words and perennial wisdom. For more information visit:

www.rumipoetryclub.com
www.facebook.com/rumipoetryclub